To _____

From _____

Date _____

THINKING OF YOU

PHOTOGRAPHY COPYRIGHT © 1996 BY VIRGINIA DIXON

TEXT COPYRIGHT © 1996 BY GARBORG'S HEART 'N HOME, INC.

DESIGN BY MICK THURBER

PUBLISHED BY GARBORG'S HEART 'N HOME, INC.

P.O. BOX 20132, BLOOMINGTON, MN 55420

ALL RIGHTS RESERVED. NO PART OF THIS BOOK MAY BE REPRODUCED IN ANY FORM

WITHOUT PERMISSION IN WRITING FROM THE PUBLISHER.

SCRIPTURE QUOTATIONS MARKED TLB ARE TAKEN FROM THE THE LIVING BIBLE

© 1971. USED BY PERMISSION OF TYNDALE HOUSE PUBLISHERS, INC.,

WHEATON, IL 60189. ALL RIGHTS RESERVED.

SCRIPTURE QUOTATIONS MARKED NIV ARE TAKEN FROM THE HOLY BIBLE, NEW

INTERNATIONAL VERSION® NIV®. COPYRIGHT © 1973, 1978, 1984 BY

INTERNATIONAL BIBLE SOCIETY. ALL RIGHTS RESERVED.

JANET L. WEAVER WISHES TO THANK JOAN M. GARBORG FOR HER EDITORIAL

DIRECTION AND WENDY GREENBERG FOR HER "APPLES OF GOLD."

ISBN 1-881830-27-6

Thinking of You!

Photography by Virginia Dixon with featured sentiments by Janet L. Weaver

A cheerful friend, like a sunny day, spreads brightness all around.

The joy that you give to others is the joy that comes back to you.

....

JOHN GREENLEAF WHITTIER

When you were born, God said "Yes!"

Thinking of
you sets my
heart to
dancing.

*I think of you
as a flower in
the middle of
the meadow…
a splash of
color just where
it's needed.*

ALEXYS J. WEAVER,
AGE 9

In friendship's fragrant garden, there are flowers of every hue. Each with its own fair beauty and its gift of joy for you.

While friends are near us, we feel that all is well…. Our everyday life blossoms suddenly into bright possibilities.

HELEN KELLER

A friend is a gift whose worth cannot be measured,
except by the heart.

To love a person is to learn the song that is in their
heart, and to sing it to them when they have
forgotten.

There are so many times I've thought about you and wondered... Do you think about me too?

Peace descends softly when I remember You're always there.

Let the beloved of the Lord rest secure in him,

for he shields him all day long,

and the one the Lord loves rests between his shoulders.

....

DEUTERONOMY 33:12 NIV

We have been in God's thought from all eternity, and in

His creative love, His attention never leaves us.

....

MICHAEL QUOIST

My friend shall forever be my friend, and reflect a ray

of God to me.

....

HENRY DAVID THOREAU

Moments shared with you are refreshing streams

of Heaven's Light.

*You have a way of making
everything around you
look glorious.*

I am beginning to
learn that it is the sweet,
simple things
of life which are the
real ones after all.

Laura Ingalls Wilder

Every day under the sun is a gift. Receive it with eagerness. Treat it kindly. Share it with joy. Each night return it to the Giver who will make it bright and shiny again before the next sunrise.

You are a blessing sent from Heaven above, a huggable reminder of God's unfailing love.

When just being together is more important than what you do, you are with a friend.

The warmth of a friend's presence brings joy to our hearts, sunlight to our souls, and pleasure to all of life.

Let's stay close...it's warmer that way.

After gathering all my favorite things around me, I remembered that I still needed you to make my world complete.

When you're with a friend, your heart has come home.

I am so glad you are here…. It helps me to realize
how beautiful my world is.

....

RAINER MARIA RILKE

May God give you eyes to see beauty only the heart can understand.

You give [us] drink from your river of delights. For with you is the fountain of life; in your light we see light.

....

PSALM 36:8,9 NIV

Joy dawns in our hearts when we realize that the One who made us fills the heavens.

*Every day is
a brand new
day to delight
in each other.*

Happiness held is the seed, happiness shared is the flower.

May happiness touch your life today as warmly as you have touched the lives of others.

Friends warm the world with happiness!

Great
friendships
start with
the little
touches.

The happiness of life is made up of little things—a smile, a hug, a moment of shared laughter.

Friendship gives a voice to the heart and wings to the soul.

It's the little things that make up the richest part of the tapestry of our lives.

Those who run in
the path of God's
commands have
their hearts set free.

Great is his faithfulness;
his lovingkindness
begins afresh each day.

LAMENTATIONS 3:23 TLB

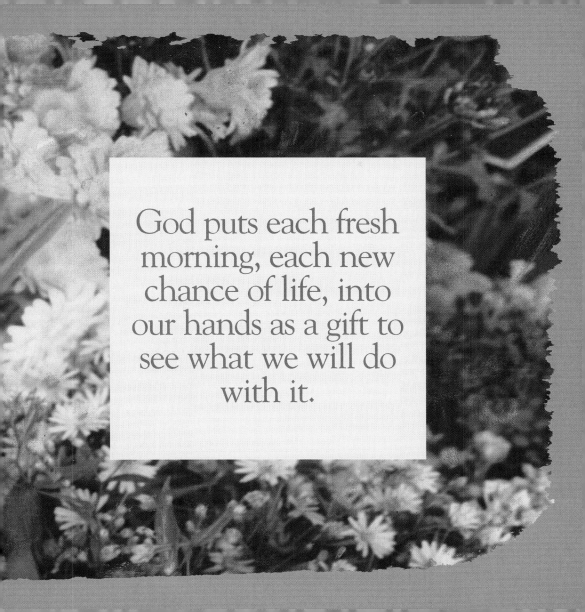

God puts each fresh
morning, each new
chance of life, into
our hands as a gift to
see what we will do
with it.

Every moment is full of wonder, and God is always present.

You have a unique message to deliver, a unique song to sing, a unique act of love to bestow. This message, this song, and this act of love have been entrusted exclusively to the one and only you.

....

JOHN POWELL, S.J.

Every person's life is a fairy tale written by God's fingers.

....

HANS CHRISTIAN ANDERSEN

*I can see
the wonder of
God's smile
resting on
you.*

Gentle thoughts of you surround me like a wreath of fragrant joy ...a potpourri of sweet memories.

Recall it as often as you wish, a happy memory never

wears out.

LIBBIE FUDIM

He surrounds me with lovingkindness and tender mercies.

He fills my life with good things.

PSALM 103:4,5 TLB